Rooster the Red Roany Pony

Written by Lauren Stanley

Illustrated by Maggie Harding

Copyright © 2019 Lauren Stanley

All rights reserved.

ISBN: 978-1-081-75317-7

DEDICATION

Rooster – You have come so far and made so many dreams come true.

Ashley, Bruce & Kenny – Thank you for molding Rooster so beautifully into the great athlete that he is.

My family – Thank you for your never-ending support.

Ian & Shane – Thank you for making sure Rooster is feeling his best every day.

On a bright sunny day in the middle of May,
a rancher let all the newborn foals out to play.
However, one foal didn't want to join the others.
He never received a name, despite being one of four brothers.
He worried his hair was the reason for his distress.
No matter what he did it always looked like a mess.

He had red and white hair
that grew just about everywhere.
But the hairs that could not be tamed
were the ones sticking straight up in his mane.
When he moved left, his hair moved right.
When he patted them down, they popped right back up into sight.

"What will my friends say?
I can't possibly let them see me this way."
The red roany pony looked into the mirror with shame.
How in the world would he come up with the perfect name?
As he stared at his reflection,
he finally began to see perfection.

"Rooster...."
He said to the mirror.
"Rooster the Red Roany Pony!"
This time he said it much clearer.

With a newfound purpose,
Rooster went back to the field.
He was excited to play with his friends
and find out what the future would yield.
"Red Rooster come here!"
As he turned, he could see a
tall slender lady standing near.

"Rooster the Red Roany Pony, it's time to come with me!
You have big things in store, just wait and see!"
The lady walked right up and cheerfully said,
as she pet the wild red hairs on his pretty little head.

"What would you like me to do?"
Rooster politely asked as she helped him slide on his shoe.
"We are going to learn to dance!"
Rooster slowly nodded as he gave her a nervous glance.

"What if I fail?"
Rooster said with a wail.
"What if I can't get over that pole?"
Rooster murmured as he almost tripped in a hole.
"What if you fly?"
The lady was quick to reply.
"What if you win?!"
The lady said with an enormous grin.

Rooster decided to dance.
He was going to work hard to make the most of his chance.
Every new move he turned,
he discovered there were unlimited skills
and knowledge to be learned.

The lady took notice of how hard Rooster was working.
However, deep in the shadows, his doubts were lurking.
His doubts were aware of how dedicated he was.
They knew he was worthy, but they hated to see him rise above.

Rooster was invited to the biggest dance of the year.
Excited as he was, his stomach twinged with fear.
Then his doubts came to life with a mind of their own.
They grabbed at his feet which made him ache and groan.

Rooster's doubts held on tight to his feet and couldn't be shaken.
The time to dance came, but he knew his confidence had been taken.
The lady saw the sadness in Rooster's eyes and asked:
"Do you think you can do it, is this something you can get past?"

Rooster knew he could do it, he knew he could dance.
It was silly to let those what-ifs block his advance.
"I love to dance and I think I'm quite good.
If I work and I work I could be the best, I know I could!"

With new faith and a new fire,
his determination to dance could never be higher.
This time he would work so hard that the doubts couldn't creep in.
There was no way he was going to let them win.
Rooster danced day and night,
with that gold trophy coming closer into sight.

One year later, the big dance came again.
Rooster was giddy with excitement
waiting for the dance to begin.
He danced and he pranced,
making the most of his second chance.

Once the last dance was through,
There was nothing left for Rooster to do.
He prayed and he waited.
When the winner was announced,
it was Rooster the Red Roany Pony who would be
forever celebrated!

BACK STORY

Rooster the Red Roany Pony is inspired by true events that involved an American Quarter Horse named Rooster. Rooster is a sweet, cautious, careful individual who possesses a personality unlike any other. When we found Rooster, we started teaching him a new event called trail, which we refer to in this story as "dancing." Rooster was, and still is, incredibly gifted in the field of "dance" and excelled at it right from the beginning. He was gearing up to be named the Greatest in the World in his first year ever "dancing." However, due to his newness to the event, he didn't shine as brightly as he could have. The next year, Rooster worked even harder and he came back stronger. That fall, he was named the AQHA World Champion. This is the story about how he overcame his own anxiety and setbacks to become the best "dancer" out there.

www.roostertheredroanypony.com

Made in the USA
Columbia, SC
13 September 2019

Gingerbread Man Traps: Christmas Family Tradition
Published by Golden Crown Publishing, LLC

www.GoldenCrownPublishing.com

© 2021 Golden Crown Publishing, LLC

All rights reserved. No portion of this book may be reproduced in any form without permission from the publisher, except as permitted by U.S. copyright law.
For permissions contact: help@GoldenCrownPublishing.com

Created by Melanie Salas
ISBN: 978-1-954648-75-3

Gingerbread Man

TRAPS

Slide for Gingerbread Man

You can't catch me!

Christmas Family Tradition

Christmas Day is almost here!

The sneaky Gingerbread Man must be near.

He will come looking
for sweet Christmas treats!

And will run off
with all he can eat!

It's time for us to build a trap.

One with a tall ladder, perhaps?

Be creative
and be smart.

Decorate with candy
or with your own art.

or the trap can be small.

The trap can be short...

or the trap can be TALL.

So, get started right away!

It's almost time for Christmas Day!

As a family, work together each year to design and build a gingerbread man trap.

You'll enjoy having this treasury of traps keepsake to remember your annual attempts to catch the sneaky little guy!

Happy Trapping!

Gingerbread Man Trap Design Plans

Year ....

Sketch your plans here!

Our Gingerbread Man Trap

Year..........

Place photo of trap here

☐ We caught him!   ☐ We didn't catch him!

Gingerbread Man Trap Design Plans

Year ....

Sketch your plans here!

Our Gingerbread Man Trap

Year ....

Place photo of trap here

☐ We caught him! ☐ We didn't catch him!

Gingerbread Man Trap Design Plans
Year ....

Sketch your plans here!

Our Gingerbread Man Trap
Year..........

Place photo of trap here

☐ We caught him!   ☐ We didn't catch him!

Gingerbread Man Trap Design Plans
Year ....

Sketch your plans here!

Our Gingerbread Man Trap

Year..........

Place photo of trap here

☐ We caught him!   ☐ We didn't catch him!

Gingerbread Man Trap Design Plans

Year ....

Sketch your plans here!

Our Gingerbread Man Trap
Year..........

Place photo of trap here

☐ We caught him! ☐ We didn't catch him!

Gingerbread Man Trap Design Plans

Year ....

Sketch your plans here!

Our Gingerbread Man Trap
Year..........

Place photo of trap here

☐ We caught him! ☐ We didn't catch him!

Gingerbread Man Trap Design Plans

Year ....

Sketch your plans here!

Our Gingerbread Man Trap

Year..........

Place photo of trap here

☐ We caught him! ☐ We didn't catch him!

Gingerbread Man Trap Design Plans
Year ....

Sketch your plans here!

Our Gingerbread Man Trap
Year..........

Place photo of trap here

☐ We caught him! ☐ We didn't catch him!

Gingerbread Man Trap Design Plans

Year ....

Sketch your plans here!

Our Gingerbread Man Trap

Year..........

Place photo of trap here

☐ We caught him! ☐ We didn't catch him!

Gingerbread Man Trap Design Plans
Year ....

Sketch your plans here!

Our Gingerbread Man Trap

Year..........

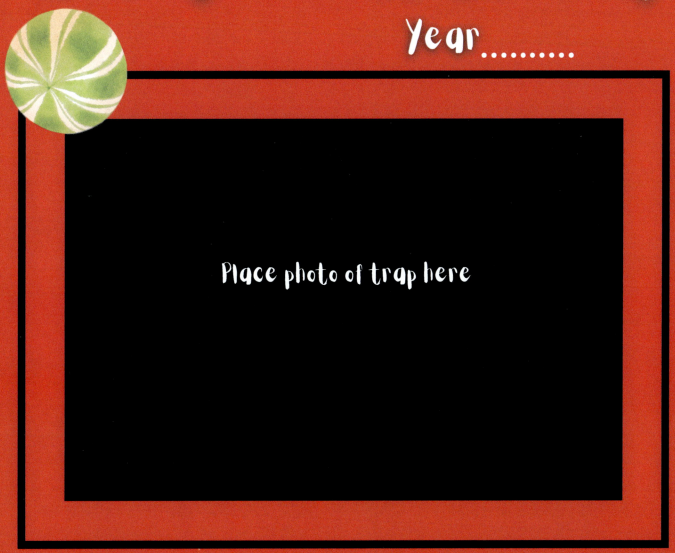

Place photo of trap here

☐ We caught him!   ☐ We didn't catch him!

Made in the USA
Las Vegas, NV
04 December 2023